# THE GHOSTLY TALES OF LEAVENWORTH AND THE CASCADE FOOTHILLS

Published by Arcadia Children's Books
A Division of Arcadia Publishing
Charleston, SC
www.arcadiapublishing.com

Spooky America is a trademark of Arcadia Publishing, Inc.

First published 2024
Manufactured in the United States

Designed by Jessica Nevins
Images used courtesy of Shutterstock.com; p. 62 Nestor Salgado/Shutterstock.com;
p. 88 Ian Dewar Photography/Shutterstock.com.

ISBN: 978-1-4671-9757-1
Library of Congress Control Number: 2024930955

Spooky America

# THE GHOSTLY TALES OF

# LEAVENWORTH

## AND THE

# CASCADE FOOTHILLS

## KATE BYRNE

Adapted from *Ghosts of Leavenworth and the Cascade Foothills* by Deborah Cuyle

arcadia
CHILDREN'S BOOKS

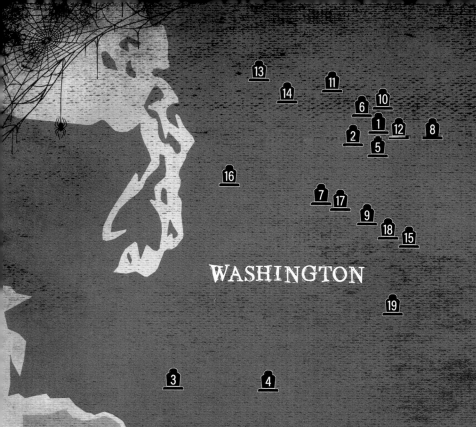

WASHINGTON

OREGON

# TABLE OF CONTENTS & MAP KEY

# Welcome to Spooky Leavenworth and the Cascade Foothills!

Welcome to the *spookier* side of Leavenworth, Washington. Of the many fascinating and unique towns I have lived in and written about, Leavenworth is one of my favorite haunts! I lived just a short drive from the German-themed city for two decades and would visit as often as I could. If you walk around the town (once called Icicle), you too will discover your own special places to explore.

Many of the historic buildings beg you to come in and look for a ghost lingering in the dark corners of the rooms. Some of the ghosts that call Leavenworth home are funny, some are secretive, and others love to move things when people are not looking! At the former Tumwater Inn, an invisible hand plays a tune from the piano in the lobby. Several Victorian ghosts walk the halls at the former Hotel Edelweiss, frightening both visitors and employees as their partial apparition appears in the rooms.

The nearby Cascade Mountains hold their own secrets. Whispers of hidden treasures and lost gold still circulate... some people roam the hills with maps and clues hoping to locate the fortune. Some of the area's beautiful historic hotels still host former guests in spectral form.

Come explore my favorite haunted locations and learn about the ghosts as we explore the colorful Bavarian village and the nearby eerie Cascade Foothills. I am sure you will enjoy my wonderfully frightening stories revealed in the *Ghostly Tales of Leavenworth*!

—Deborah Cuyle, author of
*Ghosts of Leavenworth & the Cascade Foothills*

# Haunted Hospitality

Welcome to Leavenworth's Overland Café. The year is 1911. This café is on Ninth Street and has been called the "most inviting and attractive dining room in Central Washington." The host's name is J. B. Violette, and his goal is to bring sophistication to this pioneer town. On Saturdays, there are ladies' tea parties in the afternoon. The local women wear their finest dresses and hats. Can you picture them?

They might have lace collars; long, straight skirts; and buttons down the back. They don't have many chances to dress up in this frontier town, after all. This is *the* place to see and be seen if you are a frontier lady. And the good times don't stop when the sun goes down. In fact, they just keep getting better. McDaniel's String Orchestra provides music, keeping everyone on their feet, dancing for hours. What a marvelous space!

Did we mention the food? The local paper says the café offers the best twenty-five-cent meal in town, not to mention the best service. (If you visit on Sunday, though, bring an extra quarter—it's fifty cents for Sunday dinner.) It's certainly worth it. After all, the kitchen is operated by a chef named Adolphe who came all the way from France, by way of Seattle. Even though this is a small town, its people have big dreams. Leavenworth is really becoming a boom town.

After those glamorous early days, the building on Ninth Street saw a number of changes. The café was sold and went through some hard times for a while. Then, in 1922, it reopened as the Tumwater Gateway Café. Luckily, once again, the sounds of music could be heard drifting from the café on the weekends as couples danced the night away.

Flash forward through the twentieth century. In 1987, the café and the building became the Tumwater Inn. For thirty years, it was a place where people gathered to eat, drink, and listen to live music. It did get a bit crowded at times, though . . . and not just with paying customers. Along with the living guests, it appears that at least a few spirits from the past liked the place so much, they decided to stay on.

According to the previous long-time owner, two of these spirits are a pair of ghostly sweethearts, continuing the lunchtime tradition that started during their lifetimes. As the story goes, the husband worked in a garage across the street during the 1940s or 50s. His wife would arrive at the café each day just before lunch so she could eat with him during his break. Their habit caught the attention of the café owners and patrons. They were said to be extremely devoted to each other and in love. After the man passed away, the woman continued to come to the café for lunch each day and eat alone.

The long-time owner believed the two reunited in the afterlife and continue their lunchtime ritual. Even when the café was empty, she could smell the same perfume waft through the dining room around lunchtime. She could only guess that it must be the adoring wife coming to meet her husband for their daily lunch date.

In the inn's lobby, there were frequent encounters with a musical ghost. The 1871 piano located there was available for patrons to use. Anyone who wanted to tap out a tune was welcome to try it, and various guests and visitors would try out the old instrument. Strangely, a soft tune would come from the piano even when *no one* was there! This happened at all times of day and night. The inn's former owner thought this ghost might have been a member of one of the many bands who entertained guests here in the 1920s, trying to keep the Jazz Age spirit alive from beyond the grave.

Although his job ended long ago, some say Chef Adolphe could not quite bring himself to leave the place where his food once made so many people happy. Guests at the Inn reported that items on their tables would move even though no one was touching them. Inn staff agreed that it must be Adolphe. His ghost also seemed determined to keep order in the kitchen and bar, frequently moving kitchen utensils and glassware. The former owner once rearranged the storage closet, only to later

find that the items there had been returned to their original positions. Ghosts are famously uncomfortable with change. It seems Adolphe wanted his kitchen and pantry *just* as he had left them.

The former Tumwater Inn still welcomes guests, now as the Wine Cellar. Although it has changed names many times throughout the years, its friendly ghosts seem to have stayed put.

A visit to the Wine Cellar is not your only chance to encounter ghosts in downtown Leavenworth's hospitality spots, though. Far from it! Just around the corner on Front Street is a building that once housed the Hotel Chikamin, and later, the Hotel Edelweiss. Both hotels hosted living guests . . . as well as those in spirit form.

A spectral man and woman wearing Victorian clothes were seen together in the downstairs area of the hotel, now the location of several shops. Even when the ghostly couple was not visible, guests reported feeling as if someone was watching them. Some wondered if the spirit of Mrs. Westbrook—one of the early

managers of the hotel—might still be looking out for her guests. In life, she was known to offer dance instructions. Perhaps she was trying to recruit new students?

Strange sounds once echoed in the hotel, as well. Hotel employees reported hearing hushed arguments and thumping sounds between the doors of rooms that they knew were empty. Not all ghosts are happy in the afterlife.

Now that the building is used for offices, have the ghosts moved out? It seems as though they may no longer feel like welcome guests.

# CHAPTER 2

# Gold Fever Ghosts

Have you ever heard of "gold fever"? It describes the excited or even *greedy* feeling some people get when they think about finding gold—lots of gold. The thought of "striking it rich" by finding a vein of gold underground sent people on long voyages across the world, over hills and rivers, through baking sun and snow drifts. Gold fever drove some people mad and made criminals of others. It left many, many men with nothing but broken dreams. But the quest for great riches was impossible to resist. When the very lucky few found gold in California in 1849, would-be miners from all over the world raced there, trying to be the next to strike into the ground with their pickaxes and find the "mother lode" (a rich source of gold). This time was called the California Gold Rush.

In the 1880s, gold was found in Washington's Cascade Mountains. Again, prospectors (the name given to those looking for gold) rushed to the area in search of gold. Very few found it, but those who did often kept the location secret. That's why there are so many "lost" mines in the Cascades. There are many legends connected to them.

When they had gold fever, prospectors would

do anything to get more. People who worked as partners to find gold would turn against each other and fight over their share of the strike. If rumors are true, some even went so far as to *murder* for gold.

One of the most famous stories of lost gold concerns a gold deposit found by a U.S. Cavalry officer named Captain Benjamin Ingalls. Separated from his unit and lost in the mountains, Benjamin did what he had been trained to do. He rode up to the highest point he could see—the ridge of Mount Stuart— to figure out where he was. From the top, he saw several lakes he'd never seen before. He decided to ride toward one of the lakes to check it out. As he approached it, he noticed the shimmer of minerals in the soil, including tiny flecks of gold. Benjamin quickly drew a map identifying the location of the gold. He hid the map under a boulder he was sure he could find in the future. Then, he found his way back to his unit.

Sadly, Benjamin died in an accident before he was able to make it back to retrieve his map. Or at least...that's the official story. Some think his death by accidental gun misfire might actually have been murder by a fellow soldier who had heard of Ingalls's gold discovery and wanted it for himself.

The tragic death of Captain Ingalls may be connected to some ghost sightings around Enchantment Lakes, Leprechaun Lake, Lake Vivian, and Temple Lake. Hikers have reported seeing a man dressed in an old-time soldier uniform, sitting atop a horse on a mountain hillside in the area. Others have heard shouts and calls echoing across the wooded slopes, as if comrades from the past are trying to find each other. Perhaps Captain Ingalls and his buddies are still looking for the lost treasure map.

Benjamin Ingalls is just one of many whose quest for gold seems to have ended in tragedy (and possibly, in haunting).

According to another legend, a Spanish miner started a gold mine close to the Lewis River between Mount Saint Helens and Mount Adams. Some believed the mine was located behind a waterfall, in a cavern in the mountain. For a long time, the miner made regular deposits in a bank in Oregon. Then, he disappeared. A few years later, the skeleton of a man and a mule were found near Spirit Lake. There have long been rumors of a restless ghost in this area. Some believe it's the Spanish miner, trying to keep others away so they don't discover his treasure.

In the old mining ghost town of Blewett, there is yet *another* legend of lost treasure. The story goes that in the 1890s, the wealthy son of a Scottish earl arrived in town with a treasure chest. The man was said to be a gambler who loved to play poker. One night, during a card game, he pulled out a box of gold coins to display his wealth to his friends. He was later seen by a neighbor burying something in the yard long past midnight.

Soon after, two local boys were sneaking around the man's cabin, trying to get a look at the much-talked-about local gentleman. To their shock, when they peeked through the window, they saw him lying motionless on the floor of his cabin. The boys were terrified that he was dead, but then they saw him blink. Alarmed and confused, they ran back to town to notify the local doctor. When he arrived at the scene, the doctor found that the man had had a stroke. He died not long after.

What had become of the rich man's treasure? It was never found, but some say his ghost still haunts the area where his cabin once stood.

This Scottish gentleman is just one of the treasure-seeking spirits who haunt the town of Blewett. After dark, some have heard the *clank, clank, clank* of miners' picks, although no mining has been done here for many years. Even more frightening are the strange, glowing lights. They look like old-fashioned paraffin lantern lights that people would have carried more than one hundred years ago. Many believe these are the ghosts of miners looking for treasure.

Outside Blewett, some have reported seeing the shadowy figure of a man dressed in tattered clothing. They say he moves through the fields at night, swinging what looks like a pickaxe, perhaps on an eternal quest for gold that he will never find.

# Ghosts in the Graveyard

When the railroad arrived in Leavenworth in 1893, it connected the new town to the outside world. But getting it there hadn't been easy. Laying the train track was very hard work—work that not many would want to do. Those who did take the jobs had a tough life. Some came because they couldn't find other work at home. The labor was tough on the workers' bodies. Many suffered injuries. They also missed the families they left behind. And the town was rough, with lots of gunfights and dangerous characters. Some of the rail workers never lived to see the completion of the track they built. Instead of riding home on the rails, they were laid to rest in Leavenworth. With so much hardship, is it any surprise that some of them could never quite rest peacefully?

The presence of restless spirits might explain the strange happenings in Old Leavenworth/North Road Cemetery. People who have visited after dark report seeing floating orbs of light moving eerily around the graves. The lights are said to look like the old-fashioned lanterns that rail workers once carried. Some say they have heard a *tink-tink-tink* sound, like a metal hammer hitting the metal head of a railroad spike—the same sound that would have filled the valley as the workers laid track after track. Some say they've heard whistled tunes drifting eerily through the cemetery at night, recalling the melodies that would have filled the air as the rail workers swung their axes.

It's not only the workers who have left a spectral imprint on the area. A train that used to run down the nearby track is said to continue its bygone journey in ghostly form. As long ago as 1916, a local reporter called William Chandler wrote about the ghost train in the *Leavenworth Echo*.

The story goes that one day, a young boy named John Philips was fishing from a small boat near a collapsed railroad bridge. Two years before, the bridge had failed as a train crossed over it, sending two cars into the river below. As he fished, John thought he could hear a train whistle heading in his direction. He looked up and saw a tendril of steam in the air, the kind emitted from an old-fashioned steam train. The next thing John saw was a train, steaming down the track toward the collapsed bridge. As the boy looked on in disbelief, the train rushed by in an earthshaking blur and tumbled into the river.

In the midst of the terrifying wreckage, the boy spied someone moving in the water. He grabbed his oars and rowed as fast as he could toward the wreck. As he got closer, he saw that the person in the water

was a little girl. He expected her to be crying out in distress. But instead, she seemed calm.

"Are you alright?" he called.

The little girl just laughed.

Shocked, John asked, "How can you laugh at a time like this?"

The girl reported that she was only the spirit of a girl who had died in the train crash years before. Then she asked him to scoop her up with his oars and take her back to the graveyard so she could rest in peace in the place where her body had been buried.

What a shock! John had never met a ghost before. He wasn't sure what to believe. The little girl *seemed* real. Maybe she was playing a joke on him? When John dropped her off and returned to town, he went straight to the library, where he knew he could find copies of old newspapers. He leafed through the stacks, until he finally found what he had been searching for: a newspaper story about the crash. He began to tremble. Staring out from a newspaper photograph was a picture of the little girl he had just helped. The story said that after the crash, her body had been carried downstream by the river's current, and she had drowned.

The Old Leavenworth Cemetery is not the only local graveyard with ghosts, though. And the unfortunate rail workers were not the only early settlers who worked in harsh conditions. Life was very hard for coal miners, too. Mines collapsed, explosions caused tunnels to cave in, and fires broke out. In fact,

coal mining was one of the most dangerous jobs in America between 1870 and 1914, with over 1,000 people dying on the job each year. That includes the forty-five men who died in Roslyn in 1892 in the worst mining accident in Washington history. They're buried at Roslyn Cemetery, along with ten more men who lost their lives in a mining disaster in 1909. Their deaths were a tragedy for the town, one that is still felt today. Leavenworth locals say that the ghost of a weeping woman can be heard near the graves, her sobs for her lost miner husband carried across the breeze.

Many of those buried at East Wenatchee

Cemetery lost their lives while serving their country. One long-dead soldier is said to walk the grounds at night in his army uniform. He's not alone, though. Misty white apparitions have also been spotted roaming among the tombstones. And just outside the graveyard, some have seen a dark figure walking through the orchards at night. (Perhaps an unearthly visitor who is too spooked to stay inside the gate?)

At Thorp Cemetery, many claim to have seen "Suzy," the ghost of a Native American woman. She is seated atop a white horse, and some who get close enough can hear her crying. The story goes that she lost her life nearby and has not been able to move on to the next world.

Would you be brave enough to visit one of these haunted cemeteries? Even if you didn't encounter anything spooky, you'd be sure to learn a lot about local history.

# CHAPTER 4

# Bridges, Tunnels, and Ghosts

You already know that trains are very important in Leavenworth's history. They helped make the town what it is today. But for all the good the railroad brought to the town, it was also the cause of tragedy. On one part of the track, around the Chumstick Bridge, a number of terrible accidents took place. Some began to think the area was cursed.

The first tragedy took place in 1903 when a dozen train cars derailed on this dangerous curve above the Wenatchee River. Late one night the following year, a train was traveling east, when, in almost exactly the same spot, two railroad employees noticed something strange. Jack Croak, an engineer, was working with a fireman named Wilson, whose job was to stoke the fires that operate the steam

engine. Croak's son was on the train with him that night, and he asked if he could ride in the engine with his father. For some unknown reason—perhaps his intuition—Croak told his son to sit farther back in the train.

No one is sure what happened that night, but Croak later said it felt like the ground began to give way under the train. Within seconds, a 250-foot section of the rail line began to slide down the hill toward the river. The engine tumbled into the water with several mail and passenger cars following. Croak, Wilson, and many passengers were plunged into the icy water. While Wilson later recovered, Croak— along with several rescuers and passengers— perished that night. But thanks to Croak's decision to have his son sit farther back in the train, Croak's son survived.

Just a few years later, in 1907, another fatal

train crash occurred around the same spot. It's possible one of the wheels on the train was broken, because much of the train track was torn up just behind where the crash took place. Several sleeper cars and the dining car overturned, jolting the passengers from their berths. Shockingly, another accident took place in the same area just a few weeks later. The train's conductor spied a huge boulder on the tracks ahead, but by the time he saw it, it was too late to stop a collision.

The train's engineer, Mr. McKay, and the fireman, Mr. Cahale, saw what was coming ahead on the train track. They leapt from the train, each from a different side. McKay jumped onto the ground and survived, while Cahale jumped in to the river and was never found. Perhaps it's no surprise that locals began to think this area of the track was cursed—although *who* cursed it and *why* has never been known.

There are more tragic train stories and haunting legends on the rails around the Cascade foothills. One of the most haunted is the Old Great Northern Railway Cascade Tunnel. In 1910, the deadliest avalanche in U.S. history took place here. This event became known as the Wellington Tragedy.

It was one of the heaviest snowfalls in years, with as much as a foot of snow per hour at one point. In a single day during this nine-day storm, eleven feet of snow fell. There was too much snow to keep the tracks cleared. So, two trains—Number 25 and Number 27—were delayed close to the tunnel at the Stevens Pass. The train officials needed to make a decision. Should they shelter in the tunnel or try to push forward? Each choice came with risks.

If they stopped in the tunnel, they could be trapped with snow on both sides and be unable to get out. They knew if they were enclosed in the tunnel, the fumes from the train's steam engine would also be trapped, and the passengers and crew would suffer from deadly carbon monoxide poisoning.

They decided to take their chances and move through the tunnel. But when they got close to the town of Wellington, they could go no farther. There was too much snow on the track. For six long days, the fearful passengers

stayed inside the train, keeping warm thanks to the remaining coal. Soon, however, the telegraph lines went down, and they lost communication with the outside world. Trees snapped and fell outside the train. The snow piled forty feet high.

When the temperature rose and the snow turned to rain, the existing snow at the top of the mountains became heavy. A lighting strike triggered an avalanche. This avalanche was so powerful that it snapped trees and rolled boulders. The avalanche roared down

the mountain and slammed into the train. The forceful impact sent the rail cars tumbling like toys 150 feet downhill, until they came to rest at a row of strong, tall trees. The whole avalanche took only a few moments. Many passengers and rail workers perished. The railroad closed the train depot in the town, and it never recovered. A new tunnel opened many years later.

These days, the abandoned rail tunnel is close to a popular hiking trail, the Iron Goat Trail. Those who dare to step inside it describe an eerie feeling. Some report seeing a train's headlight coming through the tunnel before it suddenly disappears. At times, the whistle of a steam train can be heard, although a train hasn't used this tunnel in decades. Some have even reported hearing the voice of a woman crying out, or the spine-tingling sound of people screaming.

Those who hike in the area with their dogs say their dogs seem afraid when they reach this particular section of the trail—whining and barking for no apparent reason. Some people say they have the creepy sensation that someone is walking behind them on the trail. When they turn, no one is there.

Teams of paranormal investigators and psychics have traveled to the tunnel and the surrounding area with sensitive ghost hunting equipment. They report many spirits here, caught in a time slip that keeps them in the place where they drew their last breath.

The place is so spooky that the park rangers assigned to this area will not approach it at night. If you happen to be in the area, you might be brave enough to check it out. But definitely stay away after dark!

# Creepy Cashmere

Imagine you've just arrived in Cashmere, a quaint town known for its fruit orchards in the surrounding countryside and famous fruit-flavored candy. On the main street, you find a vintage clothing boutique in a charming historic building. You find a cool retro shirt that you want to try on—no one else at school will have anything like it! You take the shirt downstairs to the dressing rooms, barely listening as the owner calls after you. She's saying something about the building's history as a speakeasy back in the 1930s, a time when alcohol was prohibited in America. Gangsters would sell alcohol illegally, and people would gather in secret bars called speakeasies to drink and dance. It's interesting history, but you just want to try on the shirt!

You step into the dressing room and pull the shirt on. Nice fit, but suddenly you shriek! You're not the only one looking back at you from the mirror. For just a moment, there was another face behind you! Then it was gone. You tear up the stairs, not even bothering to put your own shirt back on. The owner is waiting for you at the top of the stairs. "You look as if you've just had a fright!" You're not sure if you should mention the face in the mirror. After all, she might think you're a bit strange.

But you don't even have to tell her—she *asks*. "Did you see something—or some*one*—in the dressing room with you?" You report the terrifying vision in the mirror, but to your surprise, the owner doesn't look alarmed. "Don't worry," she says. "You're not the first to meet our ghosts."

She explains that back when there was a speakeasy here, gangsters moved alcohol from place to place in tunnels underneath the building. The tunnels were connected to other

buildings nearby, making it easy for them to go back and forth without getting caught. For whatever reason, the spirits of some of those long-ago residents of Cashmere decided to stick around. To this day, it's said their spirits *still* move around between the buildings. Shoppers feel their energy in the dressing rooms, where ghosts will sometimes show their faces in the mirror. But on some occasions, they'll get a bit bolder. Some shoppers have found that when they look in the mirror, the jewelry they were wearing is gone! When they reach for it, it's back in place. The owner also says the lights turn on and off by themselves, and that there's sometimes an unexplained heavy feeling in the air. When the owner brings her dogs to the store, they often seem to sense something and are very eager to get back outside.

The owner says she took a photo in the basement once and several spirits showed up in it. When she shared the photo with an acquaintance, the woman recognized the ghost as Kathy, a local who had died of natural causes a few years before. Maybe it's not just former gangsters hanging out here!

Paranormal investigators came to check out the building. They used sensitive equipment called EVP recorders that pick up electronic voice phenomena, or voices of the spirits. When they listened to the recordings, they heard voices asking, "What's your name?" and "You can hear us?" When the investigators asked why the ghosts wanted to scare people, the response was "Friends, friends, friends." So, maybe they really are friendly ghosts? These days, the owner greets them every morning and only asks that they hold their haunts until *after* the store closes.

This vintage clothing store is far from the only haunted location in Cashmere. There have been many ghost sightings at the Cashmere Museum, known for its collection of Native American artifacts donated by Willis Carey, a former Cashmere resident. In fact, most locals believe that Mr. Carey himself is haunting the building, still overseeing his collection.

For a small town, Cashmere certainly has a lot of ghosts! Many have reported seeing the spirit of a man near the town's railroad tracks. Local ghost hunters are almost certain they know who it is. Back in 1913, a stranger came to town and was found lying unconscious by the tracks. Although he was never positively identified, some are certain he has now become a permanent resident.

If you happen to arrive in Cashmere during the fall, you might be able to catch the town's annual festival, Scare-Crazy. It sounds spooky, but it's really about scarecrows and not frights.

# CHAPTER 6

# Annabel and the Blue Lady

The land in and around the Cascade Foothills is such a beautiful area, it's no wonder tourists have been coming here since pioneer times. The majestic mountains, forests, lakes, and outdoor recreation—it's just what most city folks need to get away from it all. They also need somewhere to stay, and that means hotels, tucked into the hills and valleys of the area. Some of the region's many historic hotels have been restored for today's guests. It seems, though, that the guests of yesteryear are present, too.

The Bush House Inn in Index was built by Clarence and Ellie Bush in 1898. Originally, the inn provided lodging for miners who arrived in the town to dig for copper. The town was new, and the railroad had arrived only a few years before. The depot was right next to the inn, so it was an ideal location. When the mines were abandoned, the town still attracted tourists drawn to its breathtaking mountain and river views. But the hotel was difficult to maintain and suffered a lot of damage during an earthquake in 1999. Though it has been beautifully restored as a ten-room hotel, it's not clear yet if the hotel's most famous resident ghost, Annabel, is happy with the update.

According to local stories, Annabel was engaged to a miner who lodged at the hotel. One day, she heard news of a deadly explosion at the mine where he worked. Desperate with grief, Annabel checked herself into the hotel and died of a broken heart. In a tragic twist, however, the miner had *not* been killed in the explosion. He returned from the mine alive ... only to find that his beloved Annabel had died. Overcome with sorrow, he took his own life. The two are considered a kind of Romeo and Juliet of the Cascades. Their love story is so tragic that it turned into a ghost story.

Those who have stayed or worked at the hotel report many hauntings. They hear footsteps in the hall when no one is present. They feel unexplained cold rushes of air. Some have smelled a waft of cologne or perfume, as if someone wearing the scent has just walked by, even though no one is there. Furniture is rearranged on its own, and lights flicker spookily. Sometimes, the sound of a woman crying can even be heard from one of the empty guest rooms.

One woman who worked in the hotel as a housekeeper was tending to a guest room when she heard a voice say, "Hello, are you cleaning my room?" The woman spun around to see who had spoken, but no one was there. She noticed that doors in the hotel opened and closed by themselves.

From outside the hotel, people have seen figures peering out from curtained windows even when the hotel was closed and empty. Paranormal investigators have come to the inn and registered a ghostly presence there.

If you'd like to visit the beautifully renovated hotel, you can stay in Annabel's room—number 9—and step into the stairwell, where her presence is most often felt. The room is decorated to reflect its spooky reputation.

Like the Bush House Inn, the Skykomish Hotel got its start back when Skykomish was a mining and timber town. Not many women lived here, and those who did had a tough life. During Prohibition days, there was a speakeasy in the hotel, where people would gather to gamble and drink. It's here where one of the town's few women met a terrible fate. It's said she had a jealous boyfriend who murdered her in the hotel. After this tragedy, her spirit never moved on.

When the hotel was in operation, there were reports of hauntings, especially in Room 32, where lights turned on and off by themselves. Some guests who dined at the hotel's restaurant also reported the feeling of being touched by unseen hands—not in a threatening way, but gently. Others reported feeling unexpected drafts through the hotel and hearing the sound of clinking silverware, even when no one was around. Hauntings were so common that hotel managers eventually called in paranormal investigators. They said they made contact with a spirit they called the

Blue Lady. Some say she is most active on what was the top floor of the hotel, in room 408. In certain variations of the story, the Blue Lady has children, and they walked the floors of the hotel with her.

Today, the building that once housed the Skykomish Hotel is home to shops on the lower floors. If you stop by, perhaps you can pay your respects to the Blue Lady. Unless, without a room of her own, she has finally been able to rest in peace.

OLMSTEAD PLACE ·1875·

**Olmstead Place**

# CHAPTER 7

# The Haunted Olmstead Place

If you visit beautiful Olmstead Place Historical State Park near Ellensburg, you will certainly learn about pioneer life. It's a picturesque old farm with a house, cabin, and barn from the 1880s. You can bring a picnic and go fishing at the creek, or in the winter, you can snowshoe or cross-country ski on the wide meadows. You can look at the vegetable gardens and historic farm equipment. You may also see—or *hear*—some of the many ghosts that have been spotted in the park.

Before settlers came to the area, members of the Yakama Nation lived on the land that's now included in the park. Historians believe that a fort and a sweat lodge were once located here. The sweat lodge was a spiritual place

with a fire at its center. Water was dripped onto rocks around the fire to create steam. This steam was part of a purification ceremony that men took part in on special occasions, such as the lead-up to a big hunt, or a young man's coming-of-age.

The Yakama people entered into a treaty with the governor of the Washington Territory in 1855 and were moved to a reservation. (A reservation is land set aside by the U.S. government for an Indigenous tribe or tribes to live on following a treaty or federal agreement.) The rest of the Yakama people's land was declared open to settlers in 1859.

The Olmstead family (Samuel, Sarah, and their three children, Clara, Philip, and Jack) arrived here in 1875, hoping to start a new life. They built a small cabin, which you can still see today, made from trees that Mr. Olmstead chopped down himself. Clara was fourteen when they arrived at the homestead. Six years later, she married George Smith, and they moved to a nearby farm. Not long after, Clara's father Samuel died.

Clara and her husband had two daughters. Sadly, Clara died when the girls were still quite young. In those days, it wasn't common for children to be raised by a single father. So, the girls went back to the Olmstead homestead to live with their grandmother, Sarah, and their uncles, Jack and Philip, who still lived there. The family built a new home in addition to the original settler's cabin. When the girls had grown up and were quite elderly, they donated the farm to the State of Washington for the creation of a state park. There was only one condition: the farm had to be preserved just the way it was when they donated it. They wanted future generations to understand more about the pioneer way of life.

The park opened to the public in 1968. The park service kept the promise to the sisters. The house was preserved much as the family had left it, with their farm equipment from over the eras remaining in the barn. In the houses, you'll find many of the family's personal items. It looks as if they've just stepped away. Or maybe . . . they haven't left at all.

Many who visit the homestead report feeling as if they are being watched. One visitor

said she smelled bread baking in the Olmstead kitchen, but the oven in the home hadn't been used in decades. Then, an even more surprising thing happened: she saw the faint outline of a woman.

Perhaps spirits from a time before the settlers arrived linger here, too. Some have reported seeing spectral figures of what appear to be Yakama people down by the park's creek. Since the area is believed to have had a spiritual significance for the Yakama, perhaps that is not such a surprise. Others have heard a woman's screams and a baby's cry in the area. Could they be the sounds of those who lived here long ago before being displaced?

A visit to the Olmstead Place Historical State Park is educational and could indeed be a fun afternoon outing. If you get the feeling that you're being watched, though, just remember you're not the first to feel that way. The spirits of the homestead's former residents don't mean any harm. They only wanted to make sure that future generations were aware of them and their way of life. Their ghosts might just be hanging around to make sure their wishes are honored.

# Tom Cypher's Engine

The railroad brought many settlers to Central Washington and helped make it what it is today. Hundreds of tracks crisscrossed the area, bringing passengers and cargo to remote communities, connecting them to Seattle and the rest of the world. When cars became the main means of transportation, many of the towns were abandoned, becoming ghost towns. The *click-clack-click* of the trains went silent, too. The tracks were abandoned and covered with weeds. These places feel a little haunted. But one local legend tells of a track that was truly haunted by the ghost of a conductor named Tom Cypher.

It was back in 1892, when rail travel was at its peak in Central Washington. From the Northern Pacific Line to the Great Northern Railroad and the Central Washington Railroad, the rails were busy. At this time, engineer

J. M. Pinckney traveled the Northern Pacific line. His routes frequently took him from the coast eastbound to the Cascades. During these long journeys, he passed the time by telling stories with the others traveling in the engine room, the conductor and the fireman, who continuously fed the coal engine's fire to keep it going. Usually, they told happy stories. But sometimes, they got into the stories of all the frightening things they'd seen on the rails.

Train wrecks. Carriages overturned. Trains colliding with some animal or unfortunate soul who'd crossed the track at the wrong time. As the men regaled each other with stories, the train approached Eagle Gorge, known to be one of the most terrifying parts of the track in the Cascades. In this place, there had been *dozens* of accidents. The conductor suddenly jumped up and grabbed the engine's controls. He jolted the screeching brakes into position and the train came to a stop.

"What is it?" Pinckney cried. He was wondering if all the frightening stories had made the conductor jumpy.

The conductor's face expressed his true terror. "It happened just a few feet from here," he muttered.

"What did?" Pinckney replied.

"Two years ago, right here," the conductor said. "This is where Engineer Cypher died."

Passengers had begun to come forward into the engine room to see what had happened. The conductor seemed to snap out of a trance. "Let's get moving again," he said.

"Are you alright?" Pinckney asked the conductor.

"Certainly," the conductor said. But Pinckney could tell something was off.

Moments later, the conductor slammed on the brakes again.

"There! Look there! Don't you see it?" the conductor cried.

Pinckney looked down the track and broke into a cold sweat. In horror, he realized there was a train on the track that they would certainly hit if they didn't brake. In fact, it was already too late. They were too close. The men braced for impact ... but the violent crash never came.

After a moment, the conductor seemed to calm down. Once again, he restarted the train.

"What's going on?" Pinckney cried in panic.

"It's not a real train coming," the conductor said. "I think ... it's Tom Cypher's engine."

"Not a *real* train?" Pinckney sputtered.

The conductor nodded solemnly. "Engine Number 33. The one Tom Cypher crashed two years ago. You've always got to look out for it when you get to the gorge."

"What on earth are you talking about?" Pinckney demanded. He had heard of the horrific accident. In 1890, the train had derailed and tumbled into the gorge, killing all aboard. He kept staring at the engine ahead on the tracks, and he noticed it was running silently, which was strange—trains at that time were usually quite noisy. There was steam coming from its smokestack, though, and the headlight alternated red, green, and white lights.

"Anyone who travels this track knows about Tom Cypher's engine," the conductor said. "I've seen it myself more than ten times."

"But the train crashed two years ago!" Pinckney protested.

"It did," said the conductor. "But that doesn't mean Tom has stopped driving his engine."

For miles and miles, the conductor pushed forward, and Tom Cypher's engine did, too, always staying just a short distance ahead. When they rounded a curve, Pinckney was finally able to get a look inside the engine car and spotted the faint form of a conductor. Pinckney shivered at the sight. Was it Tom Cypher's ghost?

When the train approached a small station, the operator warned the crew to stay back from the engine ahead. *Could he see it, too?* Pinckney wondered.

Pinckney went to the train's telegraph machine and typed out a telegraph to the upcoming station. "Has Engine 33 arrived?" he asked. Soon after, he got a reply: Yes, it had, and its fuel was exhausted. None of it made any sense.

"When we get back," the conductor told Pinckney, "don't tell anyone about seeing the train. It's bad luck."

But Pinckney couldn't help it. He asked around and found that the train had *indeed* arrived at a nearby depot with no conductor on board . . . before suddenly disappearing into mist. Locals had seen the train chugging down the tracks, too. He tempted fate by telling the story to a reporter for the *Seattle Press-Times*, the only person to save the phantom train story for future generations.

# CHAPTER 9

# The Spooky Saloon and other Roslyn Stories

When you picture an old frontier town saloon, what do you think of? Gunfights, card games, and lots of rough characters hanging around? That's probably a good description of the Brick Saloon in Roslyn, although it wasn't old back in those days. Today, the Brick Saloon has the distinction of being the oldest continuously operating bar in Washington State. But even when it was built in 1889, it was distinct.

The saloon was a success from the start, so the owners decided to rebuild a bigger, fancier saloon in the same spot in 1898. It was made of more than 45,000 bricks and included a bar imported from England! The most special part of the bar was its twenty-three-foot-long "running water spittoon." This was a kind of trough, or open water pipe that ran along the bottom of the bar. Back in those days, the men who worked in Roslyn were pretty dirty and smelly when they stopped at the saloon after work for a beer. The spittoon was there so they could spit their chewing tobacco into the water instead of on the floor. Ewww! It sounds yucky, but it actually helped keep the bar a lot cleaner. Like other bars in the Cascade Foothills, The Brick would not have been able to serve alcohol during Prohibition... at least not legally. Also, like other places, there were tunnels underneath the bar to move illegal alcohol in and hide it.

In the old days, a big-time saloon like this had a piano, and The Brick still has one today. Sometimes, it plays when no one is around. The owner thinks it must be the spirit of a past bar patron who liked to tickle the ivories (play the piano) and still manages to from beyond the grave. Remember those rough frontiersmen who liked to spit tobacco in the spittoon? They might still be around, too! Sometimes, people report a wafting scent of tobacco in the air, even when no one close by has a pipe. The spirits here seem to be enjoying themselves— laughter and clinking glasses have been heard even when the bar is closed.

But just who *are* these spirits

who've stuck around so long after the bartender's "last call"? Employees have seen the shadowy figure of a cowboy, which makes sense since many cowboys would have come to the Brick Saloon to kick back and have a good time. That doesn't explain the little girl ghost who has been seen here, though. Perhaps she was related to the owners?

While the ghosts in The Brick seem to be in good spirits, the ghostly miners near the town and its twenty-five graveyards seem much sadder.

Many believe these spectral figures are the victims of one of the terrible mining accidents that took place here in 1892. A tremendous explosion rocketed through one of the mines, blocking its entrance. Rescue workers tried to save the forty-five men trapped inside. But the air was so poisonous that the rescuers started becoming ill and had to leave. To make matters worse, there were additional cave-ins in other parts of the mine, making rescue efforts even more dangerous. In the end, only one miner lived to tell the tale. And sadly, seventeen years later, there was yet another terrible explosion that took the lives of nearly a dozen more men.

Paranormal researchers have found evidence of ghostly activity at the entrance of Roslyn's abandoned mines.

Could it be that the ghosts of these unfortunate miners still haunt the place where they were laid to rest? Some believe so. Roslyn's twenty-five cemeteries (divided by nationality and trade) are considered some of the most haunted places in Washington. There have been voice recordings of ghostly sounds in a number of cemeteries here.

Even though the last mine closed in 1962, locals say they can sometimes detect the smell of burning coal in the area. What do you think? Is the smoky smell just a strange coincidence? Or ... might this be a sign of past tragedies that can't be forgotten?

Central Washington University

# The Haunted Halls of Central Washington University

Go Wildcats! That's a cheer you'll hear throughout the year coming from the fields and stadiums of Central Washington University. But some say if you're in a certain dormitory, it's a crying ghost you'll hear.

CWU is a big public university in Ellensburg that opened in 1891 as the Washington State

Normal School. The school specialized in educating teachers, and many students still come here for that reason. This beautiful campus is known for its mix of historic and modern buildings. The school's oldest dormitory is Kamola Hall, built in 1911. If the stories are true, it's also home to Lola of Kamola, a ghost who has been haunting it for decades.

There are many stories about Lola, but the most common one is that she was a student at the school in the 1940s, during World War II.

Some say she had been in love with a boy who went away to the war and was killed in action. The pain of the loss was too much to bear, it's said, and Lola took her own life in the dorm. Others say she was a former student who just came back to relive the happy times she had at the school. Whatever the truth, Lola has had countless encounters with current students and staff.

A photographer who works at the school was putting together a photo story about Lola. He hired a model to dress in a 1940s wedding

gown, and they went to the attic where Lola's life was rumored to have come to an end. They took a lot of photos inside the attic, with the model striking spooky poses. But things got even spookier when the photographer developed the film! First, he discovered that two of the rolls were all black—*no images*—which did not make sense considering all the photos they'd taken. As the photographer developed the third roll, he saw it had a strange fog and weird marks all over the film. Then, he noticed something truly frightening: In one of the photos taken in the hall, the photographer saw a ghostly figure. He wondered if his camera was broken, but all the photos he'd taken outside on the same day were fine. He even had the film checked by the film company. There was nothing wrong with it.

For years, students have reported spectral apparitions in the hallways of the dorm. Music begins to play when nothing has been switched on, and doors open and close on their own. There have also been eerie reports of a woman crying when no one is around. Some students report seeing shadows disappear into walls or feeling as though someone is in the shared bathroom with them, when no one is there.

After the dorm underwent renovation in 2002, reports of hauntings increased. It's said that ghosts don't like change.

Lola may not be the only ghost on campus, though. In Room C-37 of Barto Hall dormitory, there have been reports of a haunting. Students who lived in the room said they heard noises impossible to account for. A shadowy male figure was seen in the doorway. There have also been reports of hauntings in Beck Hall.

What do you think? Would you want to share your college dorm with a ghost? It would be tough to get your schoolwork done

in a haunted dormitory, don't you think? But the dedicated students of Central Washington University get it done, ghosts and all. Now *that's* something to cheer about!

# CHAPTER 11

# Shadowy Shorty

Are you ready for the spookiest show in Yakima? Head to the Capital Theater. You'll have to wait for the performance on stage to end, though, because that's when the *real* shivers start! It's not until the living actors exit the stage that the theater's resident ghost, Shorty, comes out.

The Capital Theater was built in 1920 to showcase touring and local vaudeville performances, a kind of entertainment popular in the early twentieth century, featuring song, dance, and comedy. With its decorative façade and curved awning, the theater makes a striking impression outside, and inside it's even grander. Elegant frescoed ceilings and curtained box seats—it made quite a statement in Jazz Age Yakima!

Soon, the theater began to play silent movies, and then "talkies," or movies with sound. In the 1930s, it's believed a stagehand who went by the nickname of Shorty began to work here. According to local stories, Shorty fell in love with an actress performing at the

theater. But she didn't share his feelings. Tormented by his broken heart, Shorty died in the theater. But though his life may have ended, his spirit never left! Through the decades, theater staff and patrons began to notice strange things happening in the theater. The toilets would flush on their own (and this was before automatic toilets!). Backstage props would be moved around or disappear entirely. Faint whispers could be heard backstage or in other areas of the theater. Theater staff started to make a connection—Shorty was behind all this mischief. Shorty's most frequent trick was to lock or unlock the door to his "office" in the

theater's organ loft, reachable only by a ladder. Sometimes, he would transport important papers from other parts of the theater into this space, so the staff would have to climb up the ladder to retrieve them.

Ushers at the Capital Theater reported they felt like someone was following them, even when nobody else was around. One theater patron said when she took a photo of the cast during curtain call, a shadowy figure appeared in the picture with them. Slightly more frightening is the report of the audience

member who stood up to leave ... but didn't have a lower body!

As times changed, the theater's former glory faded. It was not well maintained and fell into disrepair. In the 1970s, the Capital burned down, but it was later rebuilt. Shorty's office was removed after more renovations in 2010, but the door to it remains backstage even to this day. It seems no one wanted to risk Shorty's revenge!

# A Ghostly Goodbye

A visit to Leavenworth and the Cascade Foothills is full of so many incredible sights. From the high peaks of Mount Saint Helens to the pristine waters of the Enchantment Lakes, the beauty of nature is always around you. In these forgotten ghost towns, you'll learn a lot about history. And in places like Leavenworth, you can experience the charm and excitement of a Bavarian village right in Central Washington.

Exploring this scenic wonderland, you'll find spectral traces of those who came before and helped to make Central Washington the place it is today. As you travel the twisty mountain roads and stop in small towns and bigger cities like Yakima and Ellensburg, remember that you are not alone. Many former Washingtonians are right there with you. Those who built the railroads, mined copper used all over the world, and felled timber for homes and buildings are still here in spooky

spirit. But don't be frightened. Most of Central Washington's ghosts are quite harmless and simply haven't figured out that it's time to move on. After all, who wouldn't want to spend eternity in this truly unique and special place? Just accept them as part of the journey and remember: Like the fortunate few who struck gold in these magnificent mountains, if you happen to have an encounter with the ghosts of Leavenworth and the Cascade Foothills . . . consider yourself lucky!

**Kate Byrne** grew up listening to stories about banshees, fairies, and ghosts in grand Irish houses. She loves hearing and telling spooky, supernatural stories and is always on the lookout for a good haunted house, a ghostly graveyard, and shape-shifting creatures.

Check out some of the other *Spooky America* titles available now!

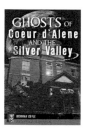
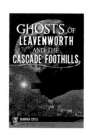
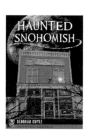
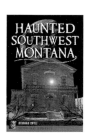

*Spooky America* was adapted from the creeptastic *Haunted America* series for adults. *Haunted America* explores historical haunts in cities and regions across America. Here's more from the original *Ghosts of Leavenworth and the Cascade Foothills* author, Deborah Cuyle: